Worship
BAND
Play-Along

DRUMSET EDITION   *Volume 1*

Holy Is the Lord

T0039905

Recorded and produced by Jim Reith at BeatHouse Music, Milwaukee, WI

Lead Vocals by Tonia Emrich and Jim Reith
Background Vocals by Jim Reith and Jana Wolf
Guitars by Mike DeRose
Bass by Chris Kringel
Piano by Kurt Cowling
Drums by Del Bennett

ISBN-13: 978-1-4234-1715-6
ISBN-10: 1-4234-1715-1

HAL•LEONARD®
CORPORATION

7777 W. BLUEMOUND RD. P.O. BOX 13819 MILWAUKEE, WI 53213

Visit Hal Leonard Online at
www.halleonard.com

Holy Is the Lord

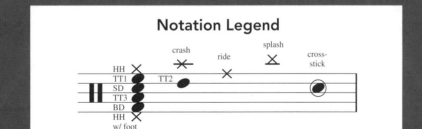

Notation Legend

Agnus Dei

Words and Music by Michael W. Smith

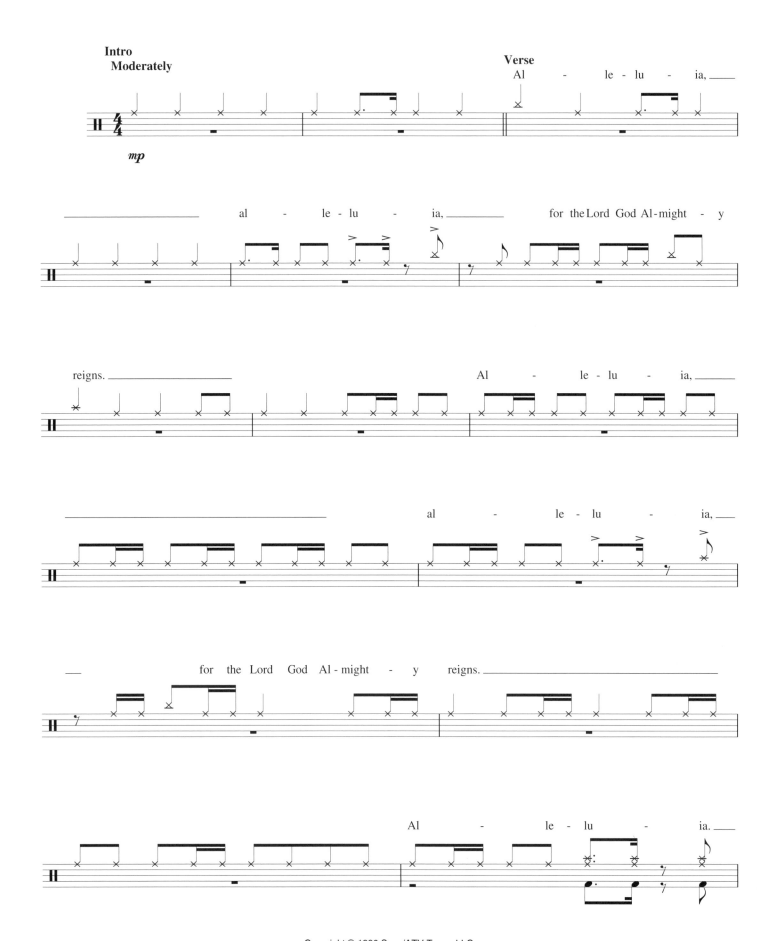

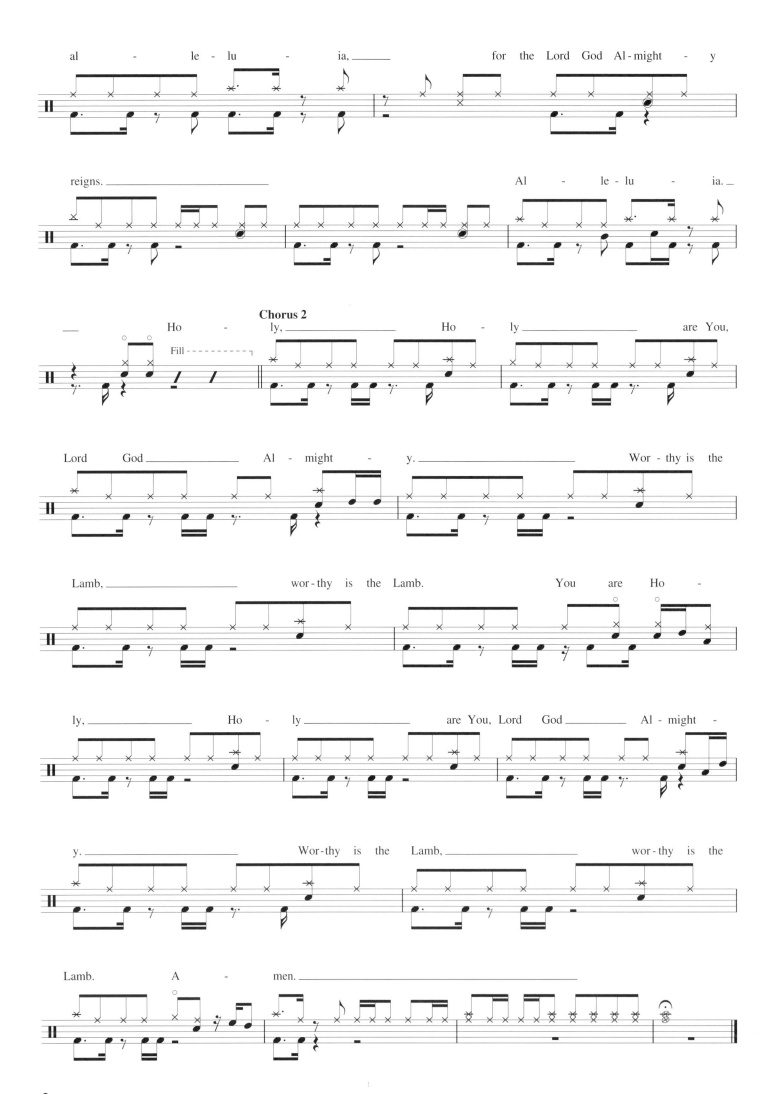

God of Wonders

Words and Music by Marc Byrd and Steve Hindalong

Verse 2

Be Unto Your Name

Words and Music by Lynn DeShazo and Gary Sadler

Holy Is the Lord

Words and Music by Chris Tomlin and Louie Giglio

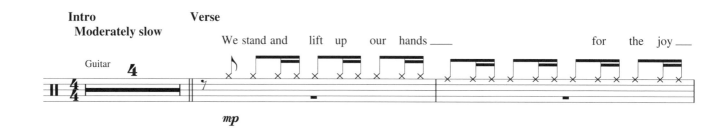

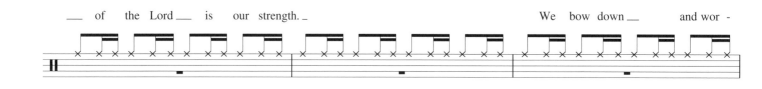

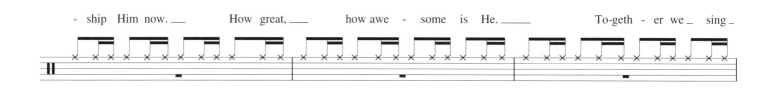

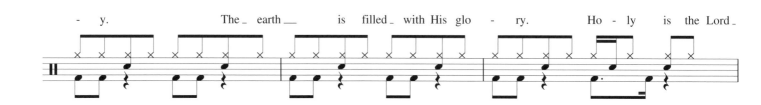

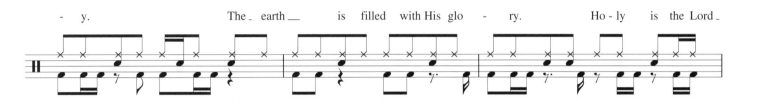

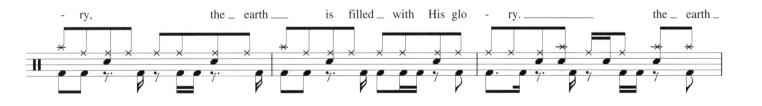

It Is You

Words and Music by Peter Furler

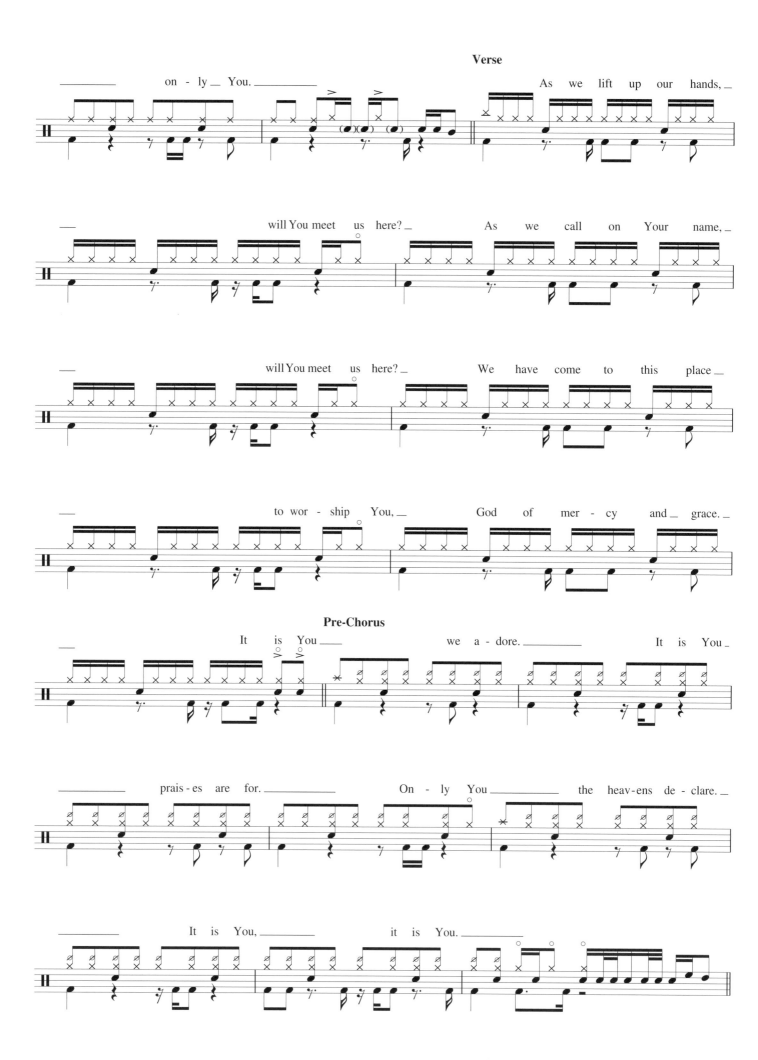

Chorus

You Are Holy
(Prince of Peace)

Words and Music by Marc Imboden and Tammi Rhoton

Open the Eyes of My Heart

Words and Music by Paul Baloche

Chorus

Chorus

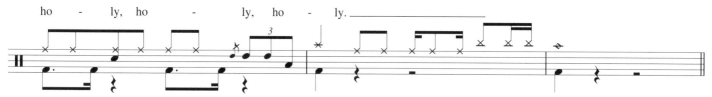

Verse

- ly, _____ ho - ly, ho - ly, ho - ly, _____ I want to

see You. _____ Ho - ly, ho - ly, ho - ly, _____

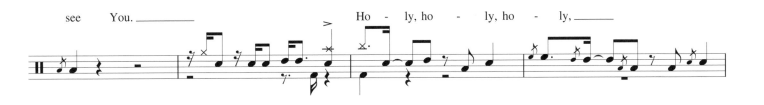

ho - ly, ho - ly, ho - ly, _____ ho - ly, ho - ly, ho - ly, _____ I want to

simile

Tag

see You. _____ I want to see You, _____ I want to

see You, _____ I want to see You, _ oh, _____

_____ I want to see You. _____

We Fall Down

Words and Music by Chris Tomlin

AGNUS DEI

MICHAEL W. SMITH

Key of **G Major, 4/4**

VERSE:

Gsus2 G   C/G G   C/G   G
      Al   - le - lu - ia

G   C/G G   C/G   D/G C/G
Al - le - lu - ia

       D/G   **C/G G**
For the Lord God Almighty reigns

G   C/G G   C/G   G
Al - le - lu - ia

G   C/G G   C/G   D/G C/G
Al - le - lu - ia

       D/G   **C/G G**
For the Lord God Almighty reigns

G   C/G G   C/G   D/G C/G
Al - le - lu - ia

CHORUS 1:

C/G   D/F♯   G
Ho -   ly

D/F♯   G(add2)
Ho - ly

      C/G G   Em   D
Are You, Lord God Almight - y

      C(add2)
Worthy is the Lamb

      C
Worthy is the Lamb

C   D   Gsus2
A -   men

(REPEAT VERSE)

CHORUS 2:

C/E   D/G   G
Ho -   ly

D/G   G
Ho - ly

      C/G G   Em   D
Are You, Lord God Almight - y

      C(add2)
Worthy is the Lamb

      C(add2)
Worthy is the Lamb

         G
You are ho - ly

D/G   G
Ho - ly

      C/G G   Em   D
Are You, Lord God Almight - y

      C
Worthy is the Lamb

      C
Worthy is the Lamb

C   D   Gsus2
A -   men

BE UNTO YOUR NAME

LYNN DESHAZO and GARY SADLER

Key of **A Major, 3/4**

INTRO:

A E Bm F#m D Asus A Esus E

VERSE 1:

A   E   Bm   F#m
We are a moment, You are forever

D   A/C# G   E
Lord of the ages, God before time

A E Bm   F#m
We are a vapor, You are eternal

D   A/C# G   Esus E
Love everlasting, reigning on high

CHORUS:

F#m D A/C#   A
Holy, Holy, Lord God Almighty

F#m D A   E
Worthy is the Lamb who was slain

F#m D A/C# E
Highest praises, honor and glory

Bm F#m   Esus E
 Be unto Your name

Bm F#m   Esus E
 Be unto Your name

VERSE 2:

A   E   Bm   F#m
We are the broken, You are the healer

D   A/C# G   E
Jesus, Redeemer, mighty to save

A   E   Bm   F#m
You are the love song we'll sing forever

D A/C# G   Esus E
Bowing before You, blessing Your name.

(REPEAT CHORUS 2X)

TAG:

Bm F#m   Esus E
 Be unto Your name

Bm F#m   Esus E (hold)
 Be unto Your name

GOD OF WONDERS

MARC BYRD and STEVE HINDALONG

Key of **G Major**, 4/4

VERSE 1:

Dsus   Em7   Csus2
Lord of all creation

Dsus   Em   Csus2
Of water, earth and sky

Dsus   Em   Csus2
The heavens are Your tabernacle

Dsus   Em   Csus2
Glory to the Lord on high

CHORUS:

G   Dsus D
God of wonders beyond our galaxy

      Am7 Csus2
You are holy,   holy

   G   Dsus D
The universe declares Your majesty

      Am7 Csus2
You are holy,   holy

Csus2   Csus2(add♯4)
Lord of heaven and earth

C   Csus2(add♯4)
Lord of heaven and earth

VERSE 2:

Dsus Em7   Csus2
Early in the morning

Dsus   Em   Csus2
I will celebrate the light

Dsus Em7   C
And as I stumble in the darkness

Dsus   Em7   Csus2
I will call Your name by night

(REPEAT CHORUS)

BRIDGE:

Am7   Cmaj7
Hallelujah to the Lord of heaven and earth

Am7   Cmaj7
Hallelujah to the Lord of heaven and earth

Am7   Cmaj7
Hallelujah to the Lord of heaven and earth

Am7   Cmaj7
Hallelujah to the Lord of heaven and earth

Dsus   D

CHORUS:

G   Dsus D
God of wonders beyond our galaxy

      Am7 Csus2
You are holy,   holy

   G   Dsus D
The universe declares Your majesty

      Am7 Csus2
You are holy,   holy

Csus2   Csus2(add♯4)
Lord of heaven and earth

C   Csus2(add♯4)
Lord of heaven and earthC

C(add2)   Csus2(add♯4)
Lord of heaven and earth

HOLY IS THE LORD

CHRIS TOMLIN and LOUIE GIGLIO

Key of **G Major, 4/4**

INTRO (GUITAR ONLY):

G Csus2 D

G Csus2 D

VERSE:

G   Csus2   D
We stand and lift up our hands

     G/B   Csus2   D
For the joy of the Lord is our strength

G   Csus2   D
We bow down and worship Him now

G/B   Csus2   D
How great, how awesome is He

     A7sus   Csus2
Together we sing

CHORUS:

     G/B Csus2 Dsus D
Holy is the Lord God Almighty

  Em7 Csus2   Dsus
The earth is filled with His glory

D   G/B Csus2 Dsus D
Holy is the Lord God Almighty

  Em7 Csus2   Dsus D
The earth is filled with His glory

  Em7 Csus2   Dsus D
The earth is filled with His glory

(REPEAT VERSE & CHORUS)

BRIDGE:

  G   D/F♯
It's rising up all around

     F   C
It's the anthem of the Lord's renown

  G   D/F♯
It's rising up all around

     F   C
It's the anthem of the Lord's renown

        A7sus Cadd2
And together we sing

     A7sus Cadd2
Everyone sing

(REPEAT CHORUS)

(REPEAT LAST LINE OF CHORUS)

END ON G

IT IS YOU

PETER FURLER

Key of **G Major, 4/4**

INTRO:

Em C D   Em C D

VERSE:

Em   C   D
As we lift up our hands, will You meet us here

Em   C   D
As we call on Your name, will You meet us here

Em   C   D
We have come to this place to worship You

Em   C   D
God of mercy and grace

PRE-CHORUS:

   G   C
It is You we adore

   G   C
It is You praises are for

    G   C
Only You the heavens declare

   G   C
It is You, it is You

CHORUS:

D   C   G
And holy, holy is our God Almighty

D   C   G
And holy, holy is His name alone

D   C   G
And holy, holy is our God Almighty

D   C   G
And holy, holy is His name alone

TRANSITION BACK TO VERSE:

   G   C
It is You we adore

   G   C
It is You, only You

(REPEAT VERSE, PRE-CHORUS & CHORUS)

BRIDGE:

G   D
As we lift up our hands

     C   G
As we call on Your name

      D
Will You visit this place

    C   G
By Your mercy and grace

     D
As we lift up our hands

    C   G
As we call on Your name

      D
Will You visit in this place

    C   G
By Your mercy and grace

G   C
It is You we adore

   G   C
It is You, it is You

(REPEAT CHORUS 2X)

ENDING:

   G   C
It is You we adore

   G   C (hold)
It is You, only You

OPEN THE EYES OF MY HEART

PAUL BALOCHE

Key of **D Major**, 4/4

INTRO (FOUR BARS):

Dsus2

VERSE:

D
Open the eyes of my heart, Lord

A/D
Open the eyes of my heart

        G/D
I want to see You

        D
I want to see You

(REPEAT VERSE)

CHORUS:

       A   **Bm**
To see You high and lifted up

G   **A**
Shining in the light of Your glory

A   **Bm**
Pour out Your power and love

      G   **A**
As we sing holy, holy, holy

(REPEAT VERSE 2X)

(REPEAT CHORUS 2X)

VERSE (2X):

D
Holy, holy holy

A/C♯
Holy, holy, holy

G/B   **G**
Holy, holy, holy

        D
I want to see You

TAG (2X):

D/F♯   **G**   **D**
I want to see You, I want to see You

WE FALL DOWN

CHRIS TOMLIN

Key of **D Major, 4/4**

INTRO (FOUR BARS):

D   A Bm G(add2)

VERSE:

D   A   Bm
We fall down, we lay our crowns

     G   Em7(add4)
At the feet of Jesus

      D   A   Bm
The greatness of mercy and love

     G   G/A A
At the feet of Jesus

CHORUS:

    D/F♯ G   D/F♯ Em7
And we cry holy, holy, holy

D/F♯ G   D/F♯ Em7
We cry holy, holy, holy

Bm A G   D/F♯ Em7
We cry holy, holy, holy

Asus D Dsus A Bm
Is the Lamb

G(add2) Em7(add4)

(REPEAT VERSE)

CHORUS:

    D/F♯ G   D/F♯ Em7
And we cry holy, holy, holy

D/F♯ G   D/F♯ Em7
We cry holy, holy, holy

Bm A G   D/F♯ Em7
We cry holy, holy, holy

Asus A D   Dsus D
Is   the Lamb

CHORUS:

Em7   D/F♯ G   D/F♯ Em7
And we cry   holy, holy, holy

D/F♯   G   D/F♯ Em7
We cry holy, holy, holy

Bm A G   D/F♯ Em7
We cry holy, holy, holy

Asus A D
Is   the Lamb

A Bm G Asus A D

YOU ARE HOLY (PRINCE OF PEACE)

MARC IMBODEN and TAMMI RHOTON

Key of **G Major**, 4/4

INTRO (EIGHT BARS):

G   G/C   Dsus D Dsus2 D
G   G/C   Dsus D Dsus2 D

VERSE:

     G(add2)   *Echo:*
You are holy   *(You are holy)*

     C(add2)
You are mighty   *(You are mighty)*

     Am7
You are worthy   *(You are worthy)*

     D
Worthy of praise *(worthy of praise)*

     G(add2)
I will follow   *(I will follow)*

     C(add2)2
I will listen   *(I will listen)*

     Am7
I will love You   *(I will love You)*

D **G**   **D**   **G**
All of my days *(all of my days)*

CHORUS

(Part I and Part II sung simultaneously):

PART I

     Csus2   **Dsus**
I will sing to and worship

     Em7   **G/B**
The King who is worthy

     Csus2   **Dsus**
And I will love and adore Him

     Em7   **G/B**
And I will bow down before Him

     Csus2   **Dsus**
And I will sing to and worship

     Em7   **G/B**
The King who is worthy

     Csus2   **Dsus**
And I will love and adore Him

     Em7   **Asus** **A**
And I will bow down before Him

     C(add2)
You're my Prince of Peace

     D   **G**
And I will live my life for You.

(REPEAT VERSE)

(REPEAT CHORUS 2X)

TAG:

     Csus2
You're my Prince of Peace

     D   **G**
And I will live my life for You

PART II

     Csus2   **Dsus**
You are Lord of lords, You are King of kings

     Em7   **G/B**
You are mighty God, Lord of everything

     Csus2   **D**
You're Emmanuel, You're the Great I AM

     Em7   **G/B**
You're the Prince of Peace, who is the Lamb

     Csus2   **Dsus**
You're the Living God, You're my saving grace

     Em7   **G/B**
You will reign forever, You are Ancient of Days

     Csus2   **Dsus**
You are Alpha, Omega, Beginning and End

     Em7   **Asus**   **A**
You're my Savior, Messiah, Redeemer and Friend

     C(add2)
You're my Prince of Peace

     D   **G**
And I will live my life for You

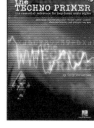